Radio Crackling, Radio Gone

*for Grace, with love, admiration
and gratitude — for your
spirit and your writing which
my mother gave me and was
my first fiction love,*

Radio Crackling, Radio Gone

LISA OLSTEIN

*June 25, 2007
Amherst*

COPPER CANYON PRESS

Printed in the United States of America

Cover art: Phyllis Berman, *Beyond Distance,* 2003. Oil on linen, 48" x 96" (six-canvas painting).

Copper Canyon Press is in residence at Fort Worden State Park in Port Townsend, Washington, under the auspices of Centrum Foundation. Centrum is a gathering place for artists and creative thinkers from around the world, students of all ages and backgrounds, and audiences seeking extraordinary cultural enrichment.

LIBRARY OF CONGRESS CATALOGING-IN-PUBLICATION DATA

Olstein, Lisa, 1972–
  Radio crackling, radio gone / Lisa Olstein.
      p. cm.
  ISBN-13: 978-1-55659-249-2 (pbk. : alk. paper)
  ISBN-10: 1-55659-249-3 (pbk. : alk. paper)
  I. Title.
  PS3615.L78R34 2006
  811'.6--dc22

                                    2006019772

98765432 first printing

COPPER CANYON PRESS
Post Office Box 271
Port Townsend, Washington 98368

www.coppercanyonpress.org

Acknowledgments

Grateful acknowledgment is made to the publications in which poems from this collection, sometimes in earlier versions, first appeared: *American Letters & Commentary, Barrow Street, Can We Have Our Ball Back?, Crazyhorse, The Cream City Review, Crowd, Denver Quarterly, 580 Split, Forklift Ohio, The Iowa Review, LIT, The Massachusetts Review, Nimrod, Orion, Poetry International, Prairie Schooner, The Pushcart Prize Anthology XXXI, Salamander, Spinning Jenny,* and *University of Massachusetts Magazine.*

Deepest thanks for readership and other forms of essential support to Dara, Noy, Michelle, Rob, Jim, Christian, Jeffrey, Liz, Lauren, Peter, Jeff, Kris, Leni, Michael, and Bill; to Michael W. and the press; to Πετρος; and to my family.

Contents

*

for my parents, Linda and Michael Olstein,

and for David

*

]
] *goatherd*
]
] *roses*

Blue Warp Black Weave

It happened because somewhere a wind died down.
I stopped loving you when a pebble hit the windshield.
A moth at the window is a symbol.

I stopped loving you when you asked me to.
A moth at the door is a sign. It would have
happened if she'd filled her pockets with stones.

It wouldn't have happened if she'd waited
one second more. I started loving you
when your sleeve caught fire. I started loving you

in a boat at sea. When it happens, how long before
a crowd accumulates, people and pigeons lining the curb?
How long before we can gauge the tensile strength

of the moment, some place where it breaks?
One man's meat, another's treason.
One man's trash, another's each-to-his-own.

One snow, suddenly birds are twice their usual size,
feather coats puffed around them, coming up
with mouthfuls of sometimes seed, sometimes snow.

The Hypnotist's Daughter

At the London Zoo a toddler falls over the rail
of the Primate World *only if you close your eyes*

and a female gorilla comes to sit by, to circle
her long dark arm around him *only this one time*

while the others stay away. The zookeeper says
she lost a baby earlier this year *only just barely*

and they've been waiting months for her tits to dry.
The boy's mother watches from above

only when I say so the thirty minutes it takes
the right person to lower the right ladder down

only as a last resort. In the interim a newscaster
whose station carries it live *only if you promise*

not to let go reports that dolphins and sometimes
certain whales rescue people stranded at sea

only when I close my eyes lift them to the air
when they need breathing or swim them close enough

to land. In the interim I imagine the span of time
from when the smooth hard snout finds me

and begins to push *only if you promise not to tell*
to when we come into view of a shore *only this once*

any shore. In the interim I pray for what should come
to come. I pray for the cat to come out from under

the floorboards *only every once in a while* to come
down from the tall maple, to come back alive

only if you say so in one piece, still in her collar.
I pray to be saved, to be sent far away, to be

4

allowed to just stay home *only another month or two*
just stay home and erase the objects in each room

with my mind while holding them in my hands
only a matter of time now. I do want to hold them

in my hands, to hold them to my lungs by way
of deep breath *only since July* and a deeper sense

of inhalation. I pray for you *only just this once*
to press out from the small veins at the back of my eyes

only you back out into the world. I pray for you
to come and sit by me *only a few more minutes now.*

Dream in Which I Love a Third Baseman

At first he seemed a child,
dirt on his lip and the sun
lighting up his hair behind him.

All around us, the hesitation
of year-rounders who know
the warmer air will bring crowds.

No one goes to their therapist
to talk about how happy they are,
but soon I'd be back in the dugout

telling my batting coach how
the view outside my igloo seemed
to be changing, as if the night

sky were all the light there is.
Now, like two babies reaching
through the watery air to touch soft

fingers to soft forehead, like blind fish
sensing a familiar fluttering in the waves,
slowly, by instinct, we became aware.

Off-field, outside the park, beyond
the gates, something was burning.
The smell was everywhere.

Another Story with a Burning Barn in It

I was on the porch pinching back the lobelia
like trimming a great blue head of hair.

We'd just planted the near field, the far one
the day before. I'd never seen it so clear,

so gusty, so overcast, so clear, so calm.
They say pearls must be worn or they lose their luster,

and that morning I happened to remember,
so I put them on for milking, finding some

sympathy, I guess, between the two.
Usually I don't sit down until much later in the day.

The lobelia was curling in the sun. One by one
birds flew off, and that should have been a sign.

Trust is made and broken. I hardly sit down
at all. It was the time of year for luna moths,

but we hadn't had any yet settling on the porch
or hovering above the garden I'd let the wild rose take.

That Magnificent Part the Chorus Does about Tragedy

There is a theory of crying that tears are the body's way of
releasing excess elements from the brain. There is a theory of
dreaming that each one serves to mend something torn, like
cells of new skin lining up to cover a hole. I'm not one to have
dreams about flying, but last week we were thirty feet above the
bay—this was where we went to discuss things, so that no mat-
ter what we decided it was only we two out there, and we'd have
to fly back together. I'm not one to have dreams where animals
can speak, but last night a weeping mare I'd been told to bridle
wanted me to save her. We discussed what was left of her ability
to take children for rides—how much trot, how much canter—
but I wasn't sure I could do it, having already bridled her and
all. I was once very brave. Once I was very brave. I was very
brave once. I boarded a plane before dawn. I carried all those
heavy bags. I stayed up the whole night before folding the house
into duffel bags. I took a curl from the base of your skull and
opened the door to the rusty orange wagon and weighed those
heavy duffel bags and smiled at the airport official. I boarded a
tiny propeller plane and from a tiny window I watched you walk
back to the rusty orange wagon. They say the whole world is
warming by imperceptible degrees. I watched the rusty orange
wagon go whizzing by.

Hypnos Is the God of Sleep

This will be the gift of salt.
This will be the gift of myrrh.
This will be the gift of take off the head
and the feet but give me the neck for soup.
This will be the gift of close your eyes,
of nearly dusk at the petting zoo,
of listen, you can't hear them anymore.

Under a boat a cricket has night all day—
warm and starless, more than dark enough.
Hawks fly and airplanes and in the marsh
a great blue heron. This is how the baby
should be put in its seat. This is how
to wipe its mouth clean. This is a cry to listen to.
This is a cry to ignore. This much
is too much. Be careful of not enough.
This is how to rock when it refuses to sleep.

You think with a slide rule and hand drawings
they could get a rocket off the ground?
If we went in '69, how come we stopped going?
The sun is the only source of light,
but shadows intersect. And where's the dust?

Dorian phrygian lydian mixolydian
locrian aeolian ionian harmonic.
Don't worry the lines, suggest the slope
and we'll guess the meaning. That's the spirit.

This will be the gift of myrrh. You take care
of what's yours. That's a star not a planet.
This will be the gift of salt. If it's cold,
give the horses their blankets. This will be
the gift of pinesap wine and cartons of milk.
If it's hot, sponge them down.

Still Early

We're always on the lookout for signs, hidden messages
in things—the curve of a pear, how long it takes to rot.
Once the flowers we bought from a curbside vendor
browned and fell in a day; once they lasted.
The first were daisies. The second were daisies.

Now this, four birds strewn so obviously
across the path of morning—one at the pantry window,
another by the door, two flying straight up, it seems, to the sky.
The neighbors have strung up their candy-colored lights.
In the field, horses are sleeping.

Regarding Days

They're going more slowly than we expected
and we expected them slow. My scarf drags on the floor,
you lift it to your face when you think I'm looking away.

It's time to set the clocks back again and send the birds on.
It's time again for them to go.
We believe we are the home they leave and come back to.

We make up contingencies and case scenarios,
we miss our prerogative, a thing in the air
we bump up against and determine to push on through.

Regarding days, they get lost beneath a woodpile;
they don't notice there's a woodpile at all.
Whispering Pines has a new shipment of ponies.

Twenty in the paddock that was empty a week ago—
small, with a temperament that comes from days spent eating grass
and years of breeding for diminutive hooves.

We're supposed to love them more than we do.
There are things we should be thankful for that we are
not thankful for, but each year it's

Look, first red leaf, Look, first white flake, first smell of wood burning
in someone's wood-burning stove. There are moments
in early morning when it feels like early morning and it is a relief.

Searching Everywhere

I never meant to say it was ordinary,
it just became so ordinary: summer
fields of unripe hay, the seamstress
looping thread through her hand again.

When I tattooed your name above my crotch
I didn't mean to imply you had to do the same.
It's the throat that tells you what to swallow,
the hand that knows when to push.

It was never said, but every day implied:
we are perpetually untested.
We contrive tests for ourselves
before the mirror, then look out

a window onto blue-black fields
where the seamstress embroiders
tiny bouquets of violets with one hand
on the back of the other.

A Great River Flows Nearby

April's first bee stumbles newly minted from its vault.
Around here we learn to mark the origins of things,
to pay attention where something comes from.

Bricklayers, electricians kneel at the dirt cusp
of a newly laid lawn. Work like prayer, or is it lunchtime
already on the job? We turn from false sweetness

on the tongue. We take a moment to determine
probability and outcome: a hive in the eaves
versus a hive in the air duct breathing out on the lawn.

We have areas of expertise; for instance,
a horse should be set running in the corner of a ring
where the proper foreleg will kick out in the proper direction.

Otherwise fall. Or run roughshod, something gnawing
the gait just left of center, stomach-side, that littered plain.
For instance, mortar. Red wires, black wires, yellow, blue.

Bricklayer, are you watching? I'll use the code
we learn around here as children—something springlike,
woeful, flashing off my teeth as I take the far turn.

I Was Mistaken

Life won't become suddenly easier
according to the crewelwork of the sky.

But I feel them: lodestar and north,
sailor's guide, sailor's siren.

At their suggestion, will I unmoor
everything I see?

It begins like a beating of wings
too close together, air turns rough,

difficult to move, difficult to breathe.
At night I bind my horse's feet in his stall.

Evening pulls too strongly at him,
he seems to lift from his straw,

he dreams he is floating, he dreams he is
the horse with the longest hair in the world.

Begin

There is no sleep, no dusk-winged mask,
no painted hood, only my porcelain
eggcup chin, your wishbone hand, only near sleep

rippling the small feathers of the brain.
Here, now, we will both begin again.
When I was born the moon was blue.

Pull in your quiet breath each time
I move closer. Let me rest
in the last place I would rest

and then not there. Begin:
moon when the wind shakes off leaves
moon of black cherries

moon of black fish
moon of long walks
moon of the home look

moon of falling leaves.
Three thousand miles down the road trees
are budding. Two cars 3,000 miles apart

on the same road—what is the difference
between when they slip into the sea?
When I am born the moon will be blue.

Through a Half-opened Door

Wednesday will be your favorite day.
You will take care when you dress.
When you undress again you will do it slowly.

You want someone to look for you
when you're not there, to imagine the way
your eyes shift, the way you hold your drink

on Saturday morning after Friday night
when you couldn't sleep. You want someone
to come, be human with you, be unforgivable.

Be as a mother is to a child splashing in the bath—
overcome, she will speak and speak until
the emotion has passed—is this why she speaks?

You like it best when someone is approaching
from a distance, moving this way, the gentle way
an ant parts grass just by moving forward.

Messages come to you sometimes by fly,
certain plain gray, red-eyed, clear-winged flies
who sit quietly, no buzzing at all.

Sometimes when strangers kiss
it's as if you're there between them,
you can feel their lips from either side.

You could swim blind across a channel
if someone guided you with whistles
timed to when you raised your head for air.

You'll be the mouth that skims the clouds
and draws in slowly—steady vapor, white breath.
Sometimes people are not meant to hide.

Dear One Absent This Long While

It has been so wet stones glaze in moss;
everything blooms coldly.

I expect you. I thought one night it was you
at the base of the drive, you at the foot of the stairs,

you in a shiver of light, but each time
leaves in wind revealed themselves,

the retreating shadow of a fox, daybreak.
We expect you, cat and I, bluebirds and I, the stove.

In May we dreamed of wreaths burning on bonfires
over which young men and women leapt.

June efforts quietly.
I've planted vegetables along each garden wall

so even if spring continues to disappoint
we can say at least the lettuce loved the rain.

I have new gloves and a new hoe.
I practice eulogies. He was a hawk

with white feathered legs. She had the quiet ribs
of a salamander crossing the old pony post road.

Yours is the name the leaves chatter
at the edge of the unrabbited woods.

Down to the Finest Particles of Every Spiraling Strand

Depending on wind and the density of morning air,
ratio of hydrogen to oxygen suspended in light

traveling the length of eight minutes from the sun,
spore after feathered milkweed spore sails east or west

or east-west across the yard. Particles of matter
making up the scent of cows in the barn mixed with hay

and the accumulating leaves of autumn await explanation.
We are still a hundred years behind the meteorologists,

and no one knows the effect of dew on vertical axis plots
of electrons buffeted by storms of solar winds or the true line

separating umbra, penumbra. A purple finch appears,
then another. Our divination tells us the sun is restless.

Garage doors open and close of their own volition.
Some people believe conceiving a child under a good aurora

increases the chance of having gifted offspring,
others that what we see in the sky are reflections,

or the glinting scales of herring off of Yellowknife
or Greenbelt or Hekla or South Slave.

*

] *in front*
] *toward*
] *loosen*

Radio Crackling, Radio Gone

Thousands of planes were flying and then
they stopped. We spend days moving our eyes

across makeshift desks, we sit on a makeshift floor;
we prepare for almost nothing that might happen.

Early on, distant relations kept calling.
Now, nothing: sound of water

tippling a seawall. Nothing: sparks
lighting the brush, sparks polishing the hail,

the flotsam of cars left standing perfectly still.
Thud of night bird against night air,

there you are on the porch, swath
of feathers visible through the glass,

there you are on the stairs where the cat fell
like a stone because her heart stopped.

What have you found in the wind above town square?
Is it true that even the statues have gone?

Is there really a hush over everything as there used to be
in morning when one by one we took off our veils?

Department for the Promotion of Virtue and the Prevention of Vice

Every place was weary and exactly the same size as before, but with more and more room as we diminished. Like some kind of accident scene, we were surrounded by those whose position in time made it theirs, too, and by all the rest who only heard something break in the darkness behind them and had no part except maybe some vague algebra of relief: perhaps this means I'll be spared today, though now the trip will be this much longer. It was a mistake, but I let him keep a spider he found. One sac and then they filled the room, drawing their webs across the door, falling from our hair. We had no choice but to kill them, one by one, when we could. Today is three years to the day since I found his bicycle among all the others propped outside the market and wound flowers around every spoke. Tonight there is good news and we will celebrate with barbers in the square and sheets burning. Tomorrow, grass soup again, and something for the donkey if we can find him in the craggy clouds and wind that each morning pull us from bed. Greetings have changed over time. No one arrives, but people vanish.

Carrier Pigeon #184

Is there snow on your mountain,
slivers of ice in the moon

reflected in the barrel
where rainwater gathers?

How many lambs are born?
How many have you decided to keep,

how many to kill? In the dark gray
beginning is it good to set aside sleep

and everything else, sit down
at a desk, stare out a window,

hold still so as not to startle the juncos
who come for the seed you lay there?

When the first flakes fall does it seem
as if they'll never add up to anything?

Are the remnants of last week's storm
still here and there on the ground

beginning to glow, have the signs
chest high around town

that say once the floodwaters
reached here begun to glow?

What Language Are They Speaking?

something brushes the lightbulb with wings

        goddamn it open your eyes   no one is home to save you

steady even if the room is sideways

            even if going dark   no one will be home for hours

look at the hall from this angle

       in this light   look at the dust on your knees

          in this instance a willingness to complain

          will be neither an advantage nor a disadvantage

it will disappear like the color of hair against the floor

     like the color of skin underwater

     like breathing in a dream

steady now   remember in the store when the oranges cascaded down

the grocer laughed   he was happy because finally there had been a rainstorm

      and some of the fruit trees

      would be saved

      but nothing could make up for last year's bees

              the ones that weren't there

      all summer quiet

The Poet's Youth Was Almost Impossibly Glamorous and Romantic

Our sheets were gathered at the corners.
It wasn't necessary, it was what we liked.
If a house burned down we built it up again, exactly as before.

The village square was like a sheep's heart kept
on display but never cut into—bifurcated, echo-chambered,
multivalved—with an endless supply of auricles

where almost anything might be hitched.
No one had to make them, the band preferred to play
in the rain, and if for years we had a certain day in mind,

nothing was set in stone. We would know it when it came
the way a caterpillar knows when the bell inside it rings,
soon a fine powder will build cities in its place,

soon wings will fan the woven ground and it will lift off
into the air making the dusty sound of a bird's wing overhead,
sometimes convincing even an old barn cat

who's climbed into the eaves to die, to step outside
and crouch down one more time in her hunter's pose.
I would see her from time to time when I was out

changing clothes in the garden, fumbling
with my buttons each time someone arrived,
so no one would see me in the same dress as another.

Bloom

There are canisters of kerosene
burning a path across the ice
taken from the kitchen store
and put there in two long rows—

midnight-blue, penguin-starred
briefly interrupted. We live
underground because it's warmer.
We've heard news of a Great Schism

and that the Old Calendarists
have not forgotten a certain slight
and of a church infested by bees
how honey runs from the walls.

Windy Today

Intention: clear. Left at the light, straight through the light, stop at the light. Cold air like snow falling, quiet in the parking lot— laundromat neon flickering, yews cut in heroic shapes of balustrades, columns, each one a thousand needled caryatids, faces turned to the ground.

Intention: clear. Little gray clouds trucking overhead under a finer layer of gauzy stuff the sun shines through like a moon. Anything that turns or bows has done so. That which stands straight through it all is left stiff-limbed against the sky. We huddle for warmth as if in a cave made of snow. A bird lives at the center of a cave of its own feathers, little pocket of trapped air.

Intention: muddled. Losing focus at every turn. Pay attention when you're driving. Stop steering with your elbows. The danger for which you keep your hands free has passed; we must prepare for another.

Intention: wait a minute. Breath steams my lenses as if the clouds reach down with their mouths. They fill me like open air.

Intention: careful review. We're on chapter 17: the Hungarians have offered their cannon to the Byzantines; one hundred and fifty thousand Turks camp against their upper banks; they refuse it as they refused surrender and a small kingdom of Greeks; the city is divided, no patriarch sits on the throne. We know what will happen. We've read this chapter before.

Intention: liquid crystal. Snow fills the field, nothing treads upon it, not even the wind. Air hovers, waits. We wait. We'll wait here.

Carrier Pigeon #23

Does longing propel you
through the shallows, the silty

shadows? Does the water open,
swallow you whole, until

you are a mirror of the sky
and you have no memory,

no future, just the loose flesh
of waves where thousands of women

have sent off thousands of men
in dinghies long after the ferries

have been commandeered,
where every year on the day of the Epiphany

a procession marches from the church
and the priest tosses a coin to the surf

and all the young men leap
into the freezing waves to bring it back,

that glowing fleck, lost and found,
year after year, for luck?

Steady Now

In swaths of blood-soaked bandages
poppies sway across the plain.
Birds thrust down their wings,
stick out their beaks, and follow one another
until something makes them fly away—
flame-blue heads in glancing sun.

Each year even the smallest pass us
on their way south, and months later
flying north again. For them,
the heart beats fast and the body is a furnace.
For us, the body is a window, a doorstop,
a weighty parcel on the back of a mare.

Butterflies, too, pass us on their long relays to and from.
Once in an ice storm not meant for May,
we watched hundreds freeze on night branches.
In the morning they drifted like embers,
bright fragments collecting around the horses' mouths
whenever they dipped their heads to the ground.

Rumors

We heard there was something going on
down in the valley, but it meant nothing to us.
There was always something going on
down in one of the valleys and rumors sifted up
like bones in a funeral mound. On that particular day
I remember our robes seemed brighter
and several women were seen out washing their hair—
lining up by the cistern, drawing cups of rainwater
in the rain. Our food arrived by the usual
village boy; his left arm was withered and for this
his mother considered him holy and dedicated
him to us twice daily with sweet rice and a little bit
of whatever the fields were yielding. Early
through the mizzen shrouds of morning an elder came,
concerned a new dish introduced at the café
would corrupt the minds of the young,
something made of egg and small bits of meat
the owner invented from a story told by a man
with a beard and a mule pack strapped to his back.
We prayed.

I Grew Up in the Dust of Many Horses

And with every disappearance something disappeared
in me, though wise men say there is no leaving
anything behind. Dust itself so often formed the cover:
fine clouds like newborn insect swarms,

like river mist hung low on the hips of evening.
We forgot what once had been by the time it lifted,
or, more often, we fell asleep,
leather saddles still warm beneath us,

jade pebbles cooling our sunburnt lips.
Someone says this is the land of Genghis Khan.
At this, someone laughs out loud.
A mare stamps her feet above my tooled pillow.

She is used to hearing the same men speak
each night around the same green-gray fire of eyes,
but will we see her there in front of us in morning
when it is time to lift the saddles and ride?

Passport

Market fills the week: fish laid out on Monday,
vegetables Tuesday, Wednesday honey and candles,
anything made by bees, meat Thursday,

grain Friday, and over the weekend, tinctures,
powders, sometimes loose leaves.
There are fairs as well, but no animals are allowed

that can't be found in paintings on cave walls.
We're interested in the rapport one has with another,
how it compares to what the paintings show,

how it develops over years, especially
as old rivalries begin to cool. New ones arise,
arguments of heredity and birthright.

Debates are ongoing and must travel from fair
to fair so what we hear is only one facet
of a jeweled conversation. Sometimes we take sides

and continue the discussion, with sadness,
like someone studying an old passport,
long after the animals have disappeared.

Carrier Pigeon #44

When dusk comes is it feathered
like a saint's bone under glass,

like a shard of something caught between
the floorboards, out of the corner of an eye?

Is it a gathering or a dispersal
as you lie there, eyes closed,

no mirror but the sea down three hills
to the right, no dirt but the dust

fine as pastry flour, the spiders'
tidy collections of wings?

Do you see them in their filament
shawls—are you sleeping?

Man Feeding Bear an Ear of Corn

What we need is an allegory.
What we want is a parable.

What we remember is a face,
movement of hands like wings.

If God is an absence, what's missing
is blue. If God is a book, its pages

are blue. Doorways appear green.
Night is a small patch in the distance

where everything swirls inviting—
a place, from this distance, you might like

to stay for a while. An arm extends
an ear to an arm extended.

If you have a hand, place it over your heart.
This necklace will not be mistaken for its chain.

*

Having been breathed out.

A Practical Guide to Self-Hypnosis

I

Outside your window daffodils
are in their February prime.
All my magnolias are zippered
deep within fleece buds.

2

above the crystalline iron core
above the liquid alloy field
above the shifting olivine mantle
the boiling peridotite wash
above the sharp-edged plate
beneath the pale iridescence of gasoline scum
beneath the seaweeded harbor water
the silt resting on the rocks
beneath the rocks and the mud they've settled into
and three feet of sand and five feet of clay:
a temple frieze—procession of women
carrying wheat and oil-filled jugs—
beneath the marble slab:
the impression of an olive branch

3

beneath your eyes beneath your lids below your brow beneath
the corneal waters beneath the iris beneath the vitreous flow
behind the vacancy of the pupil behind the macula behind the
nerve root before the brain wall:

4

Swim out too far in the bay.
Cast an invisible net before you.
With one part of your mind
pretend it's not there; with another,
begin a list of things that pass through—
lake water, stream water, mountain water,
rain off the bridge to Trastevere,
to Ankara, to Herring Cove, birds that dive
for their prey, wet shoes in a bag,
crabs, seedpods swollen with water.

5

perfect fourth
major third
major seventh
minor third
pull off
one four five
one six two five one
not in open position
two five one
two dominant
sustain grace note
root position
diminished whole
diminished strum
decay

cast on
pass slip stitch over
wool forward
wool back
drop stitch
slip stitch
barrel stitch
knit one through
drawing through
draw the first over
the second
twist stitch
carry stitch
moss stitch
hyacinth blossom

center board down
coming about
hard about
wind is luffing the sail
close haul
center board knot:
figure eight
sheet knot: *figure eight*
boom knot: *the rabbit*
comes up out of the
hole goes around the
tree and back down
into the hole
center board up
center board down

6

something blue

        water or a dress or the walls of a room

    one kiss at least

           each time, disguised: a different quality of sunlight

           a different window

                      in a different room

7

Donkey
in a burned-out
poppy field
leaning out
over a stone wall
in morning,
keeping its distance
at night,
never braying,
never looking
too long
into the goat
or the pasture,
empty field
of rocks and bramble
moonlight hits
first as it passes
over the black
rim of trees.

8

sound is earth beneath a set of wheels
entering from the left still half a mile away

lift of sand along the shoulder
headlight silhouettes of oleander and fir

silence is still half a mile to the right
darkness resettling over lemon trees

9

There is a house at the top of a hill where eagles roost
—shh, let it, it's true—
above a valley of butterflies, wind chimes, broom.
The road is dirt.
February is when irises bloom,
daffodils.
There is a room at the end of a hall.
There is a room.
There is a door.
The room is a grassland, a small savanna behind the door.
It is a place where rabbits are kept without your knowing.

*

they let their wings down

In the Meantime

What seemed a mystery was
in fact a choice. Insert bird for sorrow.

What seemed a memory was in fact
a dividing line. Insert bird for wind.

Insert wind for departure when everyone is
standing still. Insert three mountains

burning and in three valleys a signal seer
seeing a distant light and a signal bearer

sprinting to a far-off bell. What seemed
a promise was in fact a sigh.

What seemed a hot wind, a not quite enough,
a forgive me, it has flown away, is in fact.

In the meantime we paint the floors
red. We stroke the sound of certain names

into a fine floss that drifts across our teeth.
We stay in the room we share and listen

all night to what drifts through the window—
dog growl, owl call, a fleet of mosquitoes

setting sail, and down the road,
the swish of tomorrow's donkey-threshed grain.

Parable of Grief

I've turned the conch shells in the window again;
finally, I think, they're positioned right against the pane:
whorl visible, fluted edge visible, ridged back.

And this year's sea lavender has faded to the washed-out
hue that should last until next summer when one day
at low tide I'll go down to the marsh and cut more.

Through the snow-splashed glass there's a man
in every field or in every field a tree that looks like a man.
Parable of gloom, parable of winter.

When a bomb explodes in a marketplace every shred
of body must be searched for—flesh of watermelon,
fingernail, heart, stone. Tomorrow we'll clear a spot in the yard,

attach a hose to the sink and pull it out through the door.
We'll let it run, let the neighborhood kids come and skate,
let the old men come and cut a hole in the ice.

Parable of want. Let them drop a line. Parable
of plenty. Let them drink soup from steaming thermoses
and leave the smell of pipe smoke behind.

Metaphor Will Get You Everywhere

No one can see it, but she has been attached
to him for years by an invisible tether

like an astronaut whose cable disappears
against the blackness of the sky he crosses

to circle back to the shell of his craft—
something came loose in liftoff,

something needs to be observed here
away from its familiar atmosphere.

Everything wobbles.
Jam jars of nectar slow-boiled on the stove.

Sugar-water sprayed onto shirtcollars.
Forgive her, she has been too busy to write.

But that is no excuse. Forgive her,
she has forgotten to whom she might write—

in her mind he was always there
like the horses in their perfect stalls,

crèche-like, an anguished painting.
Didn't they agree to call them his,

the strip of watchful eyes on the horizon?

If the Wind Shifts

Just give me a minute here
among the radishes and asparagus,
the dogs barking from two boundary lines away.
I'm waiting for the cows to rise up
on their swollen knees and speak across time
with the shapes of their bodies.
If the wind shifts, if the men who feed them
will leave the tools they've been tending
and just hold still a minute,
if the woman in the yard will forget
the stalls of painted turtles and canaries
in the alleyway where she stood
when the bomb went off, if everything
could just for one second please hold still,
we'll see if tonight they'll rise into the statues
they make when there is no moon,
white beacons in a black galaxy settling.

Small Woman with Pictograph and Thumbnail Sketch

There are certain powers I haven't learned
to master. The last time I tried to melt a doorway
using a gentle circular motion in a clockwise direction
I went weeks without the use of my palm.
Spoons remain spoons in their drawer.

Sometimes I close my eyes and suddenly
it's been a year since the last time I tried to vanish,
months and months since I managed to interrupt
the beating of my heart. I say I didn't realize,
I hardly notice the movement of night into day
but the strain has something to do with it—
the long hours of flexing it takes.

At night, in my room, I practice not breathing,
crouching down in an old aquarium
I used to keep for angelfish, bending at the waist
and tucking my head beneath the surface—
forehead touching knees. Not breathing,
I fit as much of myself as possible into the water,
like a beast with fleas in its coat burrowing into cool
evening sand while whole civilizations rise and fall.

Today Will Be Cloudy and Gray. Tomorrow It Will Rain.

A solitary sandpiper, nine evening grosbeaks,
two gadwalls and nineteen American coots,

twenty-six purple finches, a great cormorant,
a greater yellowlegs, forty green-winged teal,

six northern harriers, seven kingbirds,
forty-three sharp-shinned hawks,

a pine siskin, common snipes and sora rails,
sandpipers including buff-breasted, white-rumped, and stilt,

fifty Cory's shearwaters, ten lesser shearwaters,
one hundred unidentified shearwaters.

3/4 Ballad

In the dark of the kitchen's turned-out light
orchids bend on their pale stems: our body doubles,
the evening's shadow pair. My feet hurt.
You let out the dog—no matter how many times
she hears the same strange sound, she still
gets up to see. Do you remember the room we shared
at the top of a house and that time I slept all day?
Do you remember the rain on Seven-Mile Bridge,
how we drove thunderclapped between the Gulf
and the Atlantic knowing there were cars ahead and behind
because we saw them before they disappeared?
On Norman Island the goats drink saltwater.
First the men brought rats from their ships, then
mongooses for the rats, and later goats for something.
Then they left—the queen no longer requiring salt
from that salt pond, preferring instead a brine found
farther east—and the goats adapted, shearing the hillsides,
drinking the sea. I could see them from the boat
as it rose and fell over the famous wreck of the *Rhône*.
There's something about the way a ship has bones,
how they attract softness and color over the years.
No matter how we fill the house with breakable things,
no matter how these things come to rest, years from now
no one will drift in slow motion over what remains.

Jupiter Moon May Hold Hidden Sea

The roof is leaking but we don't mind,
we're glad for the sound, the plip of water

filling the pot we've laid on the floor.
On that first night we took a boat across a harbor.

It must have been an effort,
keeping track of me in the dark.

And in the morning, sunlight through
the east window, the air still cool.

How many times will one person imagine light
shining through one small east-facing window?

More than I would have imagined.
Each day something makes us walk out

to the sandbars and later say I walked out
to the sandbars, I put my foot down on a shore.

Dreamboat

Each night you understand a little more
the value of escape routes, water access

by way of dock and motor to slipstream,
inlet, bay, of knowing how to navigate the hidden

rise and fall of shoals beneath the waves,
as stepping through the wash of warm air

back into the house, everything turns to meet you
with the breath of what has hummed along

steadily in your absence, what says you
may come and go, but this remains,

this waits patiently: table and chair,
couch where you sit to watch the evening

hawk take up its position on the top rail
of a paddock fence in washtub light,

the cat gaze out at this instinctual prey
that would kill him fast in a clatter of talons,

the dog droop and yawn and begin
dreaming she is running fast away.

One by One Examples Line Up by the Kitchen Window

Sounds we can identify without moving:
smokestack in evening, skirt, hair.

The street wrapped in light like a ribbon.
Sounds we must lift our heads to see:

smokestack in evening, skirt, hair.
Sometimes this is what keeps a man from drowning:

the belief that he will not drown.
Sometimes it doesn't matter what he believes.

Here in the half-light, I see two of everything.
I know the distance between two points is greatest.

Whistle for yes. Hum for no.
I'll take silence to mean anything is possible.

The Butterflies Are Coming

The way I think of you is the way I think of snow
falling from the distance of a warm day:
insistent as the cat in summertime.
She hated to come in. Let her go, you'd say
opening the door just wide enough for her
to slip back through. All those nights with the moths
and the cedar beetles, they're ending again.
It's September and monarchs are flying
up and over this unmade bed back to Mexico
to rest on the long needles of the oyamel.
You never could stand to watch anything shut in
behind closed doors, but inside the tented walls
of what they'll call a butterfly palace there will be
sugar-water in the feeders and a man displaying chrysalides
at every stage of development. I can't tell them apart,
but he can. He'll explain the differences
to every school group that passes through squealing
when a blue morpho lands on a blue-jeaned leg
or when all the swallowtails are drawn to a certain
girl's yellow hair. They will flutter around her
and alight on her hair, and eventually they will leave,
even if it is only when she leaves their vaulted air,
and she will not know what to feel.

These Are the Days of Awe

The hillside ritual of green is in its final hour.
No one is criticized for caring how they look
or for not caring. Wrongs turn into bread

which we throw into the river or anything else
moving steadily away. If this is what it takes—
four hundred men walking arm in arm up the side of a mountain,

up and down until the lost hiker is found—how then,
at a roadside stand picking over gourds and Indian corn,
in a house newly disguised under a weight of leaves,

peering into a darkened store window
where dozens of birds sleep, each head pressed
into a boulder of feathers, will we be found?

Backyard Interior

Last night I dreamed people
were very interested in what I dream.

It was the subject of much debate;
I was forced to break several hearts.

I drew you near me beneath the magnolia,
a giant canopy of ferns, we sat huddled

in the quiet empty of a tobacco barn,
light leaking in. I've heard there is an eagle

cub in a roost nearby—anything that ferocious
should not be called a chick.

I've heard an unfamiliar calling.
Later, when I tell it, the story will be charming,

full of good intentions wrangling in the yard,
but really this morning I was desperate

carting the bluebird house from place to place,
trailing sparrows across the lawn.

Surely in the flashing landscape of the brain
there is a location for bravery,

for laugh ruefully but with no bitterness,
for blame yourself a little.

Negotiation

You take the mortar; I'll take the pestle,
the weight we laid five years before the door.

You take the door, its flank and hollow.
You take the hollow morning we set out;

I'll take the conch shell, the sea.
You take the sea, our kitchen window looking out on it.

I'll take the kitchen; you take the potatoes,
their rough edges, their eyes.

You take the flashlight's eye we turned skyward
to rebut the stars. I'll take the sky it travels.

You take my fear of long journeys, of talking in my sleep.
I'll take sleep and the first morning sounds

of the monastery on the hill. You take the monks;
I'll take the way they sweep the ground

before every step, the way they nurse other men's
crippled oxen through long flickering nights.

If He Doesn't Bow to It He Will Slip It In His Sleeve and Depart

Yellow river, third moon.
Carp disappear into streams of current.

If they succeed against the waterfall
they will be transformed.

They will live in the kingfisher haze of Mt. Sanpan
and send rain to the river from above.

Notes

The epigraphs at the beginning of each section are fragments of Sappho from *If Not, Winter,* translated by Anne Carson (New York: Knopf, 2002).

"That magnificent part the chorus does about tragedy" is borrowed from Sylvia Plath, *The Unabridged Journals of Sylvia Plath* (New York: Anchor, 2000).

The list of moons in "Begin" is drawn in part from James Welch's *The Heartsong of Charging Elk* (New York: Doubleday, 2000).

About the Author

Lisa Olstein was born and raised near Boston, Massachusetts. She earned a B.A. from Barnard College and an M.F.A. from the University of Massachusetts–Amherst, undertaking additional studies at the Aegean Center for the Fine Arts and Harvard Divinity School. She is the recipient of a Pushcart Prize and a fellowship from the Massachusetts Cultural Council. She is co-founder of the Juniper Initiative for Literary Arts and Action and a contributing editor of *jubilat*.

The Chinese character for poetry is made up of two parts: "word" and "temple." It also serves as pressmark for Copper Canyon Press.

Founded in 1972, Copper Canyon Press remains dedicated to publishing poetry exclusively, from Nobel laureates to new and emerging authors. The Press thrives with the generous patronage of readers, writers, booksellers, librarians, teachers, students, and funders—everyone who shares the conviction that poetry invigorates the language and sharpens our appreciation of the world.

Major funding has been provided by:

Anonymous (2)
The Paul G. Allen Family Foundation
Lannan Foundation
National Endowment for the Arts
Washington State Arts Commission

For information and catalogs:

COPPER CANYON PRESS
Post Office Box 271
Port Townsend, Washington 98368
360-385-4925
www.coppercanyonpress.org